DIET
AND NUTRITION

Patsy Westcott

RSVP
**RAINTREE
STECK-VAUGHN**
P U B L I S H E R S
A Steck-Vaughn Company

Austin, Texas
www.steck-vaughn.com

ADOLESCENCE
DIET AND NUTRITION
DRINKING, SMOKING, AND OTHER DRUGS
EXERCISE

Published by Raintree Steck-Vaughn Publishers,
an imprint of Steck-Vaughn Company

Library of Congress Cataloging-in-Publication Data
Westcott, Patsy.
Diet and nutrition / Patsy Westcott.
    p.   cm.—(Health & fitness)
    Includes bibliographical references and index.
    Summary: Explains the importance of food to maintaining good
    health and the functions performed by various vitamins and minerals.
    ISBN 0-7398-1344-7
    1. Nutrition—Juvenile literature.
    2. Diet—Juvenile literature.
    [1. Nutrition. 2. Diet.]
    I. Title. II. Series.
    QP141.W47 2000
    613.2—dc21   99-32658

Printed in Italy. Bound in the United States.
1 2 3 4 5 6 7 8 9 0 04 03 02 01 00

Acknowledgment
The author would like to thank dietitian Lyndel Costain for her advice. Any opinions are the author's own.

Picture acknowledgments:
Digital Vision cover band (middle), 13 bottom, 15 top, 16-17, 19, 23 top, 27, 28 top; The Healthy Alliance/CCH
Communications 8; Image Bank 39 (Juan Silva); Science Photo Library 14 (Adrienne Hart-Davis), 17 top left
(Gaillard, Jerrican), 18 (Sheila Terry), 20 (Tony Craddock), 21 (Quest), 25 (BSIP Laurent H. Americain), 28 bottom
(Damien Lovegrove), 32 (Clinical Radiology Dept, Salisbury District Hospital), 33 (Steve Horrell), 34 (John Bavosi),
43 (John Greim), 44 top (Dr. P. Marazzi), 44 bottom (Adrienne Hart-Davis), 45 (BSIP Edwige); Tony Stone Images
front cover (Paul Redman), 1 (Timothy Shonnard), 4 (Elie Bernager), 5 (Lori Adamski Peek), 6 (Leland Bobbe), 7
(Christopher Bissell), 10 (Ian Shaw), 12 (John Kelly), 13 top (Yann Layma), 17 top right (Christel Rosenfeld), 22-23
(Paul Chesley), 24 (Rosemary Weller), 26 (Warren Rosenberg), 30 (Dennis O'Clair), 31 (Lori Adamski Peek), 35
(Frank Siteman), 36 (Paul Webster), 37 (Ian O'Leary), 38 (Paul Redman), 40 (Steven Peters), 40-41 (Donna Day), 42
(Peter Cade); Wayland Picture Library cover band (bottom). The illustration on page 15 is by Peter Bull.

CONTENTS

WHY WE NEED FOOD

WHAT IS DIET?

Your body uses the food you eat to help you grow, to provide you with energy, and to help you fight against infection and disease. The type and amount of food that we usually eat is known as our diet. Eating a healthy, varied diet will help keep you strong and fit throughout your life. On the other hand, an unhealthy diet can lead to many problems and even shorten your life.

FOOD FOR LIFE

In order to live, you need nutrients —nourishing substances that enable the cells of your body to work. Your body cannot make most of these nutrients, so you have to get them from the food you eat. The exact amount you need depends on your age, your size, how much you are growing, whether you are a boy or a girl, and how active you are.

FOOD FOR FUEL

Another important task of food is to provide your body with energy, which you need for activities such as walking, swimming, skating, and dancing. But you also need energy for things that you rarely think about, such as breathing, digestion, keeping your heart beating, and fueling your brain. The energy in food is measured in units called calories. A slice and a half of bread contains about 100 calories. Any calories that your body does not use are stored as fat.

Left People of different ages need different amounts of food and nutrients.

Right The food you eat provides you with energy for all kinds of exercise and activity.

A BALANCED DIET

WHAT DETERMINES DIET?

People's diet varies greatly throughout the world. It depends largely on what foods grow locally, but customs, religious beliefs, regional tastes, and economics also determine what foods people eat. Whatever foods are available, the secret of staying fit and healthy lies in making sure you have a balanced diet.

WHAT IS A BALANCED DIET?

A balanced diet provides you with just the right amount of nutrients and calories. Because just one food cannot give you all the nutrients you need, the best way to make sure you get enough nutrients is to eat a variety of different kinds of food. No foods are "good" or "bad" in themselves. The key is to get a good balance.

Your religion and your culture are among the many factors that affect the food you eat. Orthodox Jews, for example, do not eat pork, rabbit, shellfish, and eels.

Always take a bottle of water with you when you exercise, particularly when it is hot, because you need to replace the water you lose when you sweat.

WATER—VITAL FOR LIFE

You can survive for a long while without food, but only for a short time without water. Water flushes waste products from your body and helps you dissolve and digest food. Lack of water can cause dry skin, dull hair, and tiredness. You lose water when you sweat and when you urinate. You need more water during and after exercise, or if you have an illness that causes diarrhea and vomiting. Water is found in food as well as drinks, especially in fruits and vegetables. A balanced diet with several glasses of water a day should give you enough.

TYPES OF NUTRIENTS

There are two main types of nutrients, known as macronutrients (macro means large) and micronutrients (micro means small). Proteins, carbohydrates, and fats are macronutrients. You need large amounts of these nutrients for growth, development, body maintenance, and energy. Micronutrients include 45 or so vitamins, minerals, and other substances that you require for many vital bodily processes. Although you only need these nutrients in very small quantities, without them the cells of your body cannot function properly.

FOOD GROUPS

Foods are classified into five different groups, based on the nutrients they provide. These are:

★ Bread, other cereals, and potatoes
★ Fruits and vegetables
★ Milk and dairy foods
★ Meat, fish, and alternatives
★ Fatty and sugary foods

If you eat foods from each of the first four groups (not the fatty and sugary foods) every day, you should have no problem staying healthy.

Fruits and vegetables
Foods in the fruits and vegetables group are a good source of carbohydrates, protein, minerals, vitamins, and fiber. Try to eat at least one food from this group at each meal and five servings every day. They make good snacks between meals too.

Bread, other cereals, and potatoes
Foods in this group provide carbohydrates, vitamins, minerals, and fiber. Try to eat at least one food from this group at every meal and at least six servings each day.

Meat, fish, and alternatives
Foods such as meat, fish, eggs, dried beans and peas, lentils, and nuts contain protein and vitamins and minerals. Try to eat two servings a day from this group.

Fatty and sugary foods
The fifth group of foods includes things such as cookies, doughnuts, potato chips, corn snacks, ice cream, mayonnaise, bottled sauces, honey, sweets, chocolate, and sweet drinks. Because these foods contain a lot of calories but relatively few nutrients, it is best not to eat them very often, and even then only in small amounts.

Milk and dairy foods
These foods, such as yogurt and cheese, provide protein, calcium, and other vitamins and minerals. You should eat three servings from this group every day.

Many different foods can provide the nutrients you need—the important thing is to make sure you enjoy what you eat.

By following these guidelines and making sure you have a good breakfast, lunch, and dinner each day, you should get a healthy, balanced diet. You can also eat two or three small snacks a day— just be sure that they are healthy ones and not "junk food." The food plate opposite illustrates the basic principles of a healthy diet.

DIETARY DOS AND DON'TS

Do
★ Enjoy your food.
★ Eat a variety of different foods.
★ Eat sufficient food to keep you at a healthy weight.
★ Eat plenty of foods rich in starch and fiber.
★ Eat plenty of fruit and vegetables.

Don't
★ Eat too many foods that contain a lot of fat.
★ Consume sugary foods and drinks too often.

FOOD IS FOR GROWTH

A good diet is crucial as you enter your teens, when you are growing taller and heavier and need extra energy and nutrients. Eating protein foods such as meat, fish, lentils, and beans helps your muscles grow and develop. Calcium, found in milk, cheese, and yogurt, is necessary for your bones to grow strong and healthy. Iron from meat, oily fish, and lentils is also vital. Red blood cells contain lots of iron, and the amount of blood in your body is constantly increasing as you grow. Iron is especially important for girls once they start having periods.

GROWTH RATES IN BOYS AND GIRLS

The growth spurt—the sudden surge in height and weight that happens during your teens—starts around age ten in girls and twelve in boys. The makeup of your body changes too. Girls put on more fat and boys lose fat. These differences mean that boys and girls need different amounts of food. If you eat according to your appetite, you will generally get enough nutrients and calories, provided you make healthy choices. To make sure you are eating the right amount, ask your doctor to check your height- and weight-gain from time to time against a growth chart.

Above The rapid increase in growth during your teens means that your energy and nutrient needs increase.

Right On these growth charts, the darker blue areas between the red lines show the range of normal weight and height at different ages. The green line in the middle shows the average height or weight. At any one age, about 50 percent of children will be above the line, and about 50 percent below it. If you measure your height and weight regularly and mark the measurements on the charts, you will get a line that shows your own growth line. Your line should run parallel to the green line. If it does not, or if it is above or below the red lines, you should consult a doctor.

DID YOU KNOW?

★ Up to the age of ten, your body consists of about 18 percent fat. During adolescence, girls' body fat increases to about 28 percent and boys' decreases to about 15 percent.

★ Your body uses around 100 calories a day simply to grow.

★ Between 11 and 14, you need about 2,220 calories a day if you are boy and around 1,845 calories if you are a girl.

★ During the growth spurt you can expect to grow an average of 9 in. (23 cm) taller and put on 44 to 57 lbs. (20–26 kg) in weight.

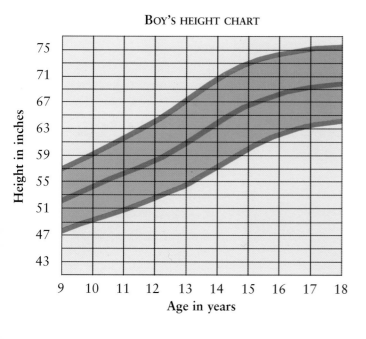

BOY'S HEIGHT CHART

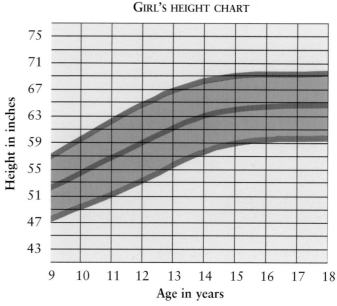

GIRL'S HEIGHT CHART

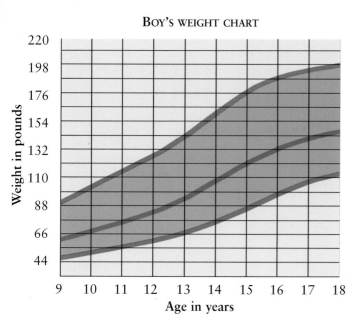

BOY'S WEIGHT CHART

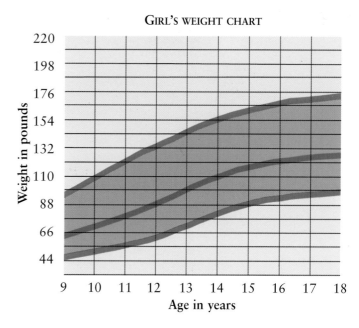

GIRL'S WEIGHT CHART

ENERGY

All types of bread contain starch, which your body breaks down to get energy.

CARBOHYDRATES

The main source of fuel for your body is a group of foods known as carbohydrates. Chemical reactions inside your body break down carbohydrates, releasing energy for your body to use. There are three main types of carbohydrates: starch, fiber, and sugar.

STARCH FOR STAMINA

Starch is found in bread, pasta, rice, cassava, potatoes, yams, and other foods. It is known as a complex carbohydrate. Your body breaks down starch very slowly, gradually releasing the energy it contains over several hours. This keeps your energy levels stable and gives you the stamina to keep going.

WHY YOU NEED FIBER

Fiber is also a complex carbohydrate. Your body does not fully digest fiber, but the fiber plays an important part in keeping you healthy. Insoluble fiber, sometimes called roughage, is found in bran (the husks of whole-grain cereals such as brown rice) and in the skin and seeds of fruits, vegetables, beans, and nuts.

TRUE OR FALSE?

An apple a day keeps the doctor away.
True. Most fruit and vegetables contain soluble and insoluble fiber. Apple peel is made up an insoluble fiber called cellulose, while apple flesh is a source of a soluble fiber called pectin. Apples also contain vitamins and minerals that help protect you against disease.

Insoluble fiber helps to prevent constipation and enables waste products from food to pass smoothly through your digestive system. It also reduces your chances of developing bowel disease.

Rice is the main source of carbohydrate for people in some parts of the world.

SOLUBLE FIBER

A second type of fiber, called soluble fiber, is partly broken down by the digestive system. It is found in beans, lentils, most fruits and vegetables, porridge oats, rye bread, and barley. It helps to lower levels of cholesterol, a substance that contributes to heart disease, and to prevent sudden increases in blood sugar, which can lead to uneven energy levels. To make sure you get the right amount of fiber—both soluble and insoluble—eat a variety of different fiber-rich foods each day, rather than just sprinkling bran on your cereal.

Candy is best eaten as an occasional treat, because it provides very few nutrients apart from high-calorie sugars.

TYPES OF SUGAR

Sugar is a simple carbohydrate, which means that your body can break it down quickly. There are many different types of sugar. Sucrose is a type of sugar used in candies, cookies, cakes, and soft drinks. Other sugars include fructose (found in fruit and honey), glucose (honey, fruit and vegetables), maltose (sprouting grains), and lactose (milk). They all give you energy, but only glucose is immediately available for your body to use. Other types of sugars must first be converted to glucose inside your body.

WHY TOO MUCH CANDY IS BAD FOR YOU

Sugar, the main ingredient of candy, can cause tooth decay. Although candy is crammed full of energy—about 375 calories per 100 grams—it contains few important vitamins and minerals. Candy is digested quickly, causing a rapid rise in your blood-sugar levels and giving you a quick burst of energy. Unfortunately, it doesn't last long, and you soon feel tired and lackluster. Candy can also kill your appetite for more nutritious food. Last—but not least—many candies contain artificial colorings that cause allergic reactions such as wheezing, headaches, and rashes in some people.

DOES CHOCOLATE GIVE YOU PIMPLES?

It is a myth that chocolate gives you pimples. Pimples and blackheads (acne) are mainly due to the hormonal changes that occur during adolescence. In fact, chocolate is one of the best sweets to eat and less liable to cause tooth decay than others. It contains some protein and minerals, as well as substances that are said to boost brain chemicals and help you feel good. It also contains caffeine, which makes you more alert. Now for the bad news: chocolate is very high in fat and calories, so it can make you put on weight. As with other candy, it is best eaten only as a treat.

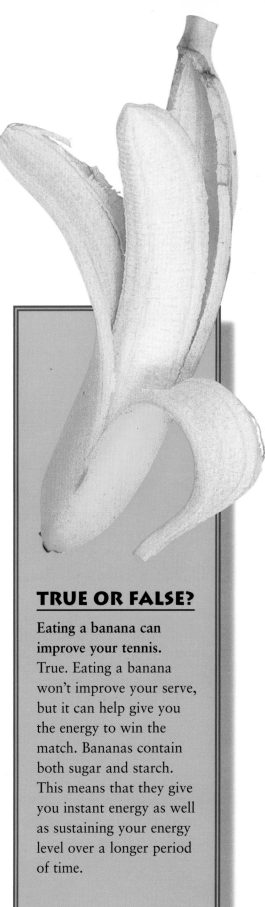

Below Too many sugary foods and drinks cause tooth decay (dental caries). Bacteria that live in the mouth use sugars for energy and produce acids that destroy teeth.

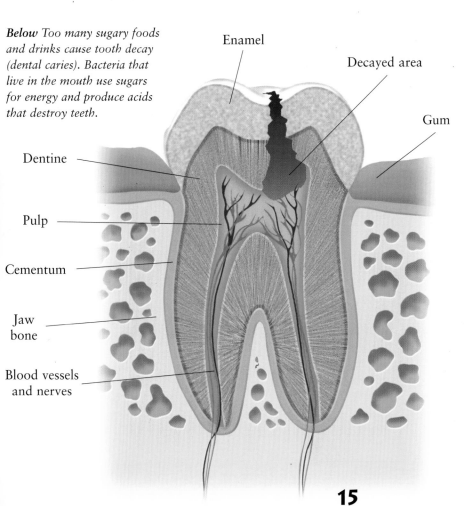

Enamel

Decayed area

Gum

Dentine

Pulp

Cementum

Jaw bone

Blood vessels and nerves

TRUE OR FALSE?

Eating a banana can improve your tennis.
True. Eating a banana won't improve your serve, but it can help give you the energy to win the match. Bananas contain both sugar and starch. This means that they give you instant energy as well as sustaining your energy level over a longer period of time.

PROTEIN

WHAT IS PROTEIN FOR?

You need protein for your body's growth, maintenance, and repair. Protein helps you have strong muscles and fight off infections. It also strengthens your hormonal system. The precise amount of protein you need varies, but if you eat a balanced diet you should get all you need. Any extra protein that you take in but do not use up will be burned inside your body to provide energy or be transformed into fat.

Below All types of fish are good sources of protein and other vital nutrients. White fish are low in fat, while oily fish provide Omega-3 fats, which research shows can help prevent heart disease.

AMINO ACIDS

Protein is one of the most complicated substances in the human body. When you digest protein, it is broken down into much simpler substances called amino acids. Your body uses these to repair muscle, skin, and other tissues and to build a strong immune system. Some of the 20 amino acids found in protein can be manufactured by your body, but eight—called essential amino acids—can be obtained only from food.

Above Shellfish, including shrimp, crabs, and lobsters, are rich in essential amino acids, which cannot be manufactured by your body.

Right Beans, lentils, chickpeas, and other types of peas and beans provide protein, but they do not contain enough of all the essential amino acids.

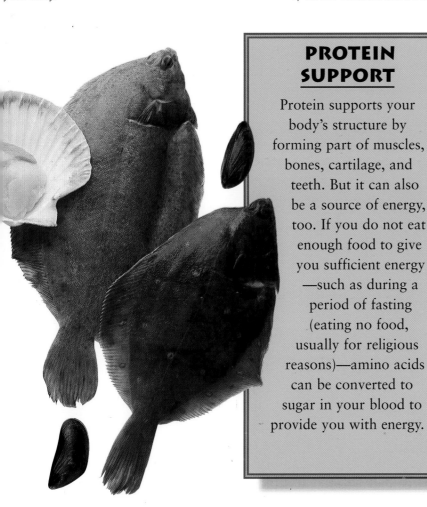

PROTEIN SUPPORT

Protein supports your body's structure by forming part of muscles, bones, cartilage, and teeth. But it can also be a source of energy, too. If you do not eat enough food to give you sufficient energy —such as during a period of fasting (eating no food, usually for religious reasons)—amino acids can be converted to sugar in your blood to provide you with energy.

TYPES OF PROTEIN

Meat, fish, shellfish, eggs, dairy products, and soya products (such as soya milk, soy beans, and tofu) contain all eight of the essential amino acids. Such foods are known as high-quality proteins. Cereals, beans (except soy beans), lentils, and nuts are proteins, but they do not contain all the essential amino acids. That is why they are often called low-quality proteins.

GETTING ENOUGH PROTEIN

If you eat meat and fish, it is easy to get all the amino acids you need because your diet automatically includes high-quality proteins.

Vegetarians who do not always eat soya products should eat a variety of different plant foods to get the right amount of protein. When you eat low-quality proteins together—for example baked beans, rice and dhal (lentil curry), rice and peas, or a peanut butter sandwich—the amino acids in them combine to provide you with protein levels similar to those found in meat. This is known as complementary eating. So if you are vegetarian, provided you eat a varied, balanced diet, you won't be short of protein.

Many vegetarians get their high-quality protein from eggs and soya products.

SOURCES OF PROTEINS

MEAT AND FISH EATERS	VEGETARIANS
Chicken	Baked beans
Turkey	Green beans
Pheasant	Soy beans and soya
Rabbit	products (e.g., tofu, miso,
Ham	soya milk)
Beef	Lima beans
Pork	Butter beans
Lamb	Hazelnuts
Salmon	Cashew nuts
Trout	Brazil nuts
Cod	Cheese
Tuna	Eggs
Swordfish	

DO ATHLETES NEED EXTRA PROTEIN?

It is sometimes said that athletes need extra protein. True, muscle is mostly made of protein, but excess protein can reduce the water content of body tissues and harm athletic performance. What athletes really need is carbohydrates for extra energy. Body-builders are different. They need extra protein to help build muscle tissue. Body-builders tend to eat more than the average person, so they naturally take in more protein. Their needs can be met by a healthy, balanced diet, without need to take protein or amino acid tablets.

If you are an athlete, you should eat plenty of starchy carbohydrate foods—rather than extra protein—to give your muscles the fuel they need to make you a winner.

FAT

THE PROS AND CONS OF FATS

Fat is the most concentrated source of energy in your diet. It provides you with twice as many calories as carbohydrate or protein. Fats help your food taste better, give it a better texture, and give it flavor and smell. Some kinds of fats contain nutrients that you need for growth and the development of tissues such as those in your brain. The layer of fat under your skin also helps you keep warm. You need to eat some fats and oils, but eating too many of the wrong kind can make you overweight.

FATS TO EAT MORE OF

Make sure your diet contains plenty of fish, vegetables, seeds, and nuts. Dress your salad with oils such as olive, soy, or sesame.

Below Fish and chips (french fries) *provide protein, carbohydrate, and fat —but don't eat them too often, as they are high in saturated fat.*

A FISHY STORY

Oily fish, such as mackerel, herring, tuna, and salmon, contain a group of fatty acids called Omega-3. These fats help the brain and eyes to develop in unborn and newborn babies. Omega-3 fats also help reduce inflammation and the tendency of blood to clot. They can be used to treat heart disease, the skin complaint psoriasis, and arthritis. Omega-3 fats are also found in walnuts and rapeseed oil.

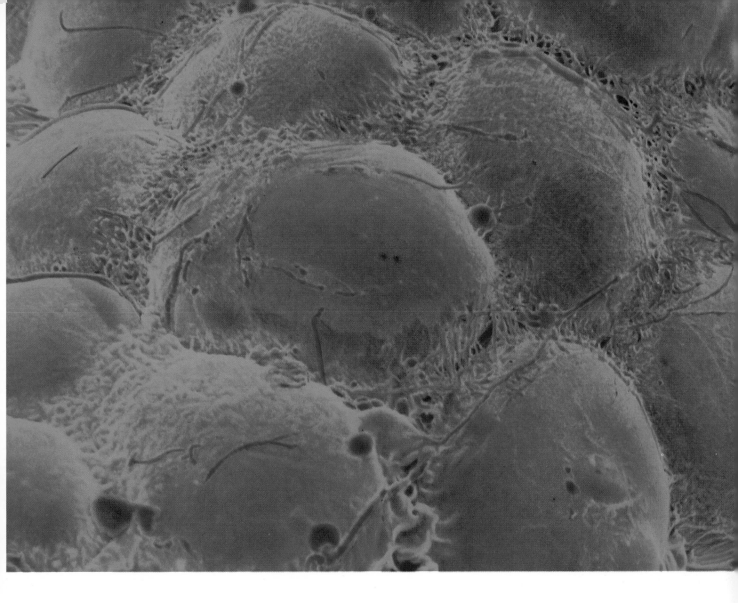

Above These are fat cells, magnified 750 times. They accumulate in a thick layer under your skin that helps keep you warm and acts as an energy store.

This will ensure that you get enough of the healthiest types of fats called unsaturated fats. You need unsaturated fats to provide you with a group of nutrients called essential fatty acids.

FATS TO EAT LESS OF

Fats that tend to be hard at room temperature, such as butter, meat fat, lard, and cheese, are called saturated fats. They come mainly from animals and animal products. Eating too many of these can increase the risk of heart disease.

To ensure you do not get an excess of saturated fats, avoid eating too many fried foods. Choose lean cuts of meat and eat more poultry, such as chicken and turkey, which are lower in saturated fats than red meats.

FATS TO EAT IN MODERATION

Cookies, pies, cakes, potato chips, fatty sauces, and mayonnaise contain trans fats. These fats, created by food processing, may also be a risk factor for heart disease, so it is wise to avoid eating too many foods containing them.

VITAMINS AND MINERALS

ESSENTIAL SUBSTANCES

The chemical processes that keep your body going rely heavily on vitamins and minerals. Although your body needs them only in small amounts and they do not provide you with energy, vitamins and minerals are still absolutely essential. Fruits and vegetables are especially rich in these substances.

Below A market in Malaysia. Fresh fruits and vegetables contain more vitamins and minerals than most manufactured or processed foods.

WHAT DO VITAMINS AND MINERALS DO?

Each vitamin or mineral has its own specific job. For example, vitamin A is good for your eyesight, vitamin C helps you fight infections, and the mineral iron helps you have healthy blood. As well as performing important jobs on their own, vitamins and minerals also work alongside each other. Vitamin C, for example, helps the body absorb and use iron.

WHY SHOULD YOU EAT UP YOUR GREENS?

Green vegetables such as broccoli, cabbage, lettuce, and spinach contain many important vitamins and minerals. They are especially rich in vitamin C. Dark-green leafy vegetables also contain a B vitamin called folic acid, which your body needs to produce new cells. A shortage of folic acid can cause anemia. Try to eat at least a portion of these every day.

Above *Green leafy vegetables, such as this lettuce, are a good source of vitamin C and the mineral folic acid.*

DID YOU KNOW?

★ Smoking increases the need for vitamin C. People who smoke should increase their daily intake of vitamin C by drinking an extra glass of fresh orange juice each day.

WATER-SOLUBLE VITAMINS

Some vitamins, such as the C and B group vitamins, are called water-soluble vitamins because they dissolve in water. Because you are constantly losing water through sweat and urine, your body cannot store water-soluble vitamins. This means that you need to eat foods containing them every day. Unfortunately, we sometimes ruin these vitamins in the process of cooking food. Boiling vegetables for too long can destroy water-soluble vitamins, so steaming vegetables is better. To be sure of obtaining these vitamins, it is a good idea to eat some vegetables raw in salads.

Salads are an important part of a healthy, balanced diet, because the raw vegetables they contain are especially rich in vitamins and minerals.

VITAL VITAMINS

VITAMIN	WHY YOU NEED IT	WHERE TO FIND IT
A	Growth	Tuna, herring, mackerel, liver, kidneys, milk, eggs, cheese, margarine, butter
Beta-carotene	May help fight against certain kinds of cancer	Carrots, broccoli, spinach, cabbage, oranges, tomatoes, red and yellow peppers, pumpkins, squash, sweet potatoes, cantaloupe
B group vitamins	Growth and development, healthy nervous system, digestion, converting food into energy	Liver, yeast extract, meat, milk, yogurt, cheese, butter, eggs, fish, whole-grain cereals, dark green vegetables, Brazil nuts, pistachio nuts, walnuts, beans, bananas
C	Healthy teeth, bones, skin; helps absorb iron	Fruits and vegetables such as peppers, citrus fruits, strawberries, blackcurrants, potatoes
D	Helps body absorb calcium and phosphorus for healthy bones and teeth	Fish liver oils, eggs, fortified margarines, tuna, salmon, sardines
E	Helps protect against heart disease	Vegetable oils, nuts, seeds, margarine
K	Needed for normal blood clotting	Green leafy vegetables, especially cabbage, broccoli, Brussels sprouts

FAT-SOLUBLE VITAMINS

Vitamins such as A, D, E, K, and beta-carotene dissolve in fat in your body and are stored in your liver and other places. Because they are fat-soluble, your body absorbs them better if you eat a bit of fat at the same time as you take in the vitamins. Having carrots (which contain beta-carotene) as part of a meal that is cooked with a dash of oil will help make your body more efficient at absorbing these vitamins.

VITAMIN DEFICIENCIES

If your body does not get enough of a particular vitamin from your diet, you may develop a deficiency disease. A severe lack of vitamin C, for example, results in scurvy, a deficiency disease that causes swollen joints and internal bleeding. Sailors used to suffer from scurvy because they could not get enough fresh food on long voyages. In developing countries, deficiency of vitamin A is linked to childhood blindness.

A dermatologist looks at a woman's face through a lens to examine a skin complaint. Vitamin C, found in most fruits and vegetables, is particularly important for healthy skin.

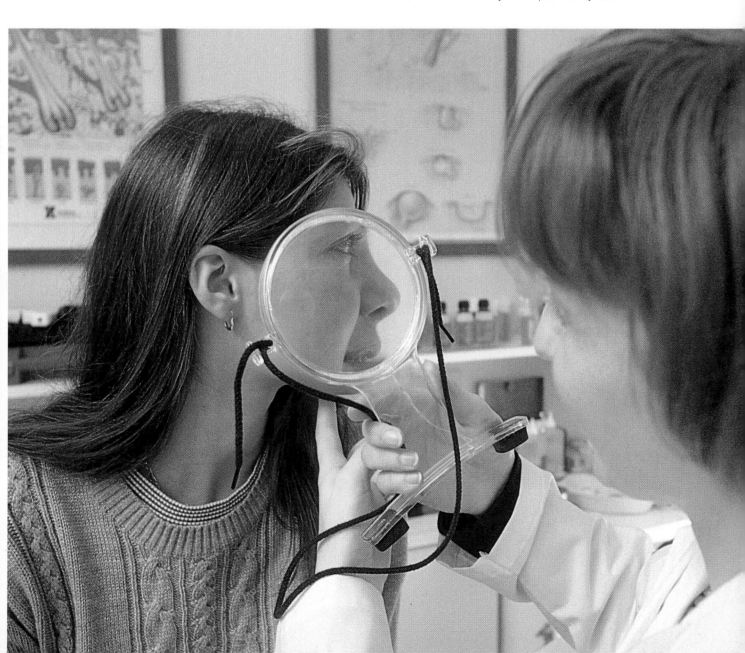

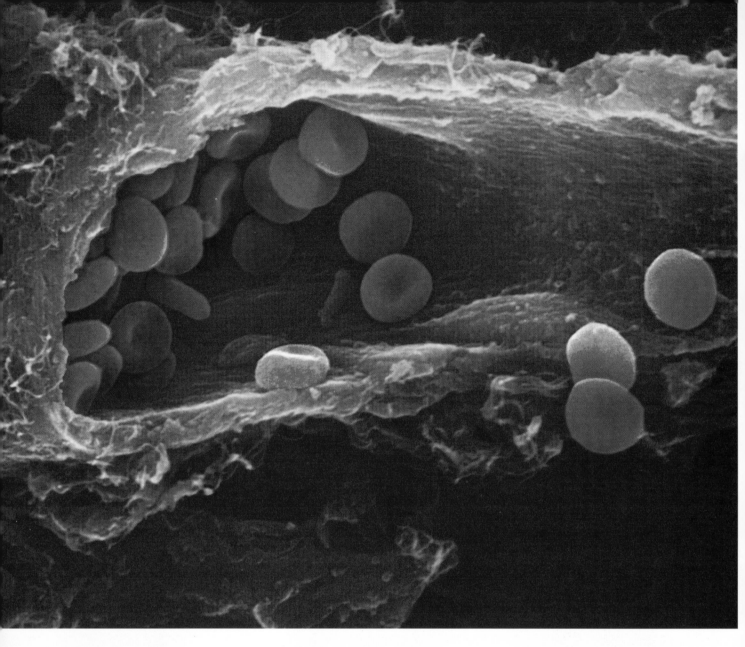

WHAT ARE MINERALS?

You need minerals to enable your body to perform hundreds of vital processes. Some minerals become part of your bones, teeth, and muscles, and some are needed for chemical reactions in your body. Other minerals help balance your body's fluid levels and regulate the acidity of your blood. Two of the most important minerals during your teenage years are iron and calcium.

HOW IS IRON IMPORTANT?

Iron is an essential part of hemoglobin, a protein found in red blood cells. Hemoglobin carries oxygen around your body and releases it wherever it is needed. There are two types of iron: one type is found in meat, fish, and poultry, while the other occurs in non-meat foods such as dark green vegetables, dried fruits such as apricots, fortified cereals, and breads.

Above Disc-shaped red blood cells passing through a vein. Iron is important for the formation of hemoglobin, the oxygen-carrying protein found in red blood cells.

ABSORBING IRON

Non-meat iron is the hardest type for your body to absorb. Vitamin C helps us absorb it, so eating an orange or drinking a glass of fresh orange juice with meals containing iron is helpful. Other substances such as tannins, which are found in tea, can block iron absorption by as much as half, so try not to drink tea with an iron-containing meal.

MINERAL DEFICIENCIES

Like vitamins, minerals are vital to the proper functioning of our bodies, so a diet that is lacking in a certain mineral can cause a deficiency disease. If your body is not getting enough iron, for example, you could develop anemia, a blood disease in which people look pale and become tired very easily.

Below Eating plenty of vitamin-C-rich fresh fruits will help your body absorb the essential mineral iron from non-meat sources, such as dark green vegetables and cereals.

WHERE DOES CALCIUM COME FROM?

Milk and dairy foods are especially rich in calcium. Having three servings a day will meet your needs. A serving is a glass of milk, a small cup of yogurt, or a matchbox-sized piece of cheese. Although calcium is also found in bread, beans, canned fish with bones, nuts, seeds, dried fruit, and green leafy vegetables, it is sometimes poorly absorbed. Eating foods containing vitamin D such as oily fish, margarine, eggs, and fortified breakfast cereals will help your body absorb calcium from these sources.

Shellfish are a good source of iodine— a key mineral for healthy growth.

OTHER IMPORTANT MINERALS

Apart from iron and calcium, other minerals that are particularly important when your body is growing are magnesium, phosphorus, and iodine. Zinc also is also important for growth and sexual development.

Milk is an especially good source of calcium, which your body needs for strong bones and healthy teeth.

MINERAL MAGIC

MINERAL	WHY YOU NEED IT	WHERE TO FIND IT
Calcium	Healthy bones and teeth, helping messages pass between nerves, blood clotting, muscle function	Milk and dairy foods, canned sardines, nuts, sesame seeds, broccoli
Chloride	Helps maintain body's fluid balance; too much is linked to high blood pressure	Table salt (sodium chloride), packaged soups, stock cubes, processed foods, ready meals, snacks such as potato chips
Fluorine	Healthy teeth and bones	Seafood, sea salt, tap water
Iodine	Healthy thyroid gland (the thyroid is involved in growth and controls energy release in the body)	Seafood, seaweed
Iron	Healthy blood, especially red blood cells	Liver, kidneys, sardines, dark green vegetables, apricots, breakfast cereals
Magnesium	Healthy bones and teeth, healthy nerves; helps muscles contract	Whole-grain cereals, nuts, dried peas and beans, sesame seeds, dried figs, green vegetables
Phosphorus	Healthy bones and teeth; helps release energy from cells; helps absorb other nutrients	Milk, cheese, meat, fish, poultry, cheese, nuts, seeds, cereals
Potassium	Helps maintain fluid balance; keeps heartbeat regular and maintains blood pressure	Bananas, avocados, potatoes, seeds, nuts
Zinc	Growth, sexual development, healthy immune system	Oysters, red meat, peanuts, sunflower seeds

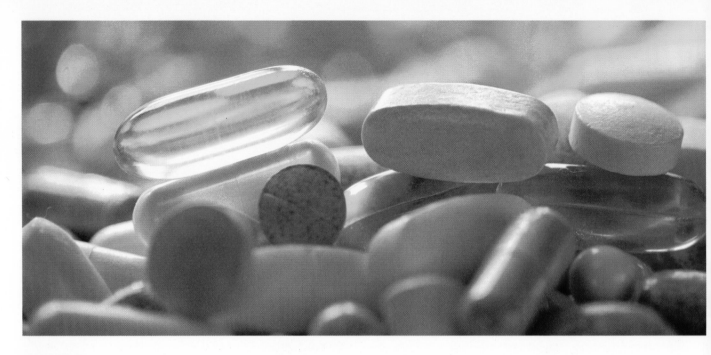

FOOD SUPPLEMENTS

If you are not getting enough nutrients from your diet, you can take food supplements, which are vitamins and minerals in pill, capsule, or liquid form. For example, if you are not eating a well-balanced diet because you are on a strict slimming regime, you could be depriving yourself of essential nutrients and may benefit from a supplement containing a balanced range of vitamins and minerals. If you are severely anemic, your doctor may prescribe a supplement of iron and vitamin C.

SUPPLEMENTS FOR VEGANS

If you eat no animal products because you are vegan, you may need a vitamin B 12 supplement, which is found naturally only in foods of animal origin. You may also need a calcium supplement, because the body does not absorb calcium very well from non-animal sources.

KEEPING YOURSELF WELL

Some nutritional experts believe that taking vitamin or mineral supplements in addition to a healthy diet can protect against certain diseases. Extra vitamin E, for example, may protect against the risk of heart disease.

SUPPLEMENT DANGERS

Some vitamin and mineral supplements are dangerous in excess. Your body cannot get rid of fat-soluble vitamins such as vitamins A and D. Too much vitamin A can damage the liver and bones and cause abnormalities in an unborn baby, while an excess of vitamin D can cause calcium to build up and damage the heart and kidneys.

Above Vitamin and mineral supplements can help if you are not getting enough nutrients from your diet. However, taking too many supplements can be dangerous.

Right Under normal circumstances, a healthy diet and plenty of energetic activity should provide you with all the strength and stamina you need, without having to take supplements.

CAN SUPPLEMENTS BUILD MUSCLES?

Ads for "high-performance" sports drinks and foods often claim that they boost your strength and muscles. Some of these products contain large doses of amino acids or vitamins and minerals. But such supplements are not helpful and may even be harmful. The best way to develop muscles is to exercise regularly and eat a well-balanced, high-carbohydrate, low-fat diet.

HEALTHY EATING FOR LIFE

FOOD AND ILLNESS

Doctors have known for some time that people who eat a diet containing lots of fatty foods run a greater risk of becoming overweight and developing high blood pressure and heart disease. In the last few years, it has also been discovered that many vitamins, minerals, and other substances in food can actively protect your body against illness and disease.

VITAMINS ARE ACE!

The vitamins beta-carotene, C, and E are often known as the ACE vitamins. The "A" in ACE refers to the fact that your body converts beta-carotene into vitamin A. Together, the ACE vitamins are antioxidants. This means that they help keep your cells healthy by mopping up substances called free radicals, which can damage your cells. Free-radical damage is linked to diseases such as heart disease, cancer, arthritis, diabetes, and cataracts (when the lenses of the eyes become cloudy).

FOOD AS MEDICINE?

Long before people knew about vitamins and minerals, doctors used food and herbs to treat illnesses. Scientists have now begun to identify a whole range of plant chemicals in food that act like medicines and help you fight serious illnesses such as heart disease and cancer.

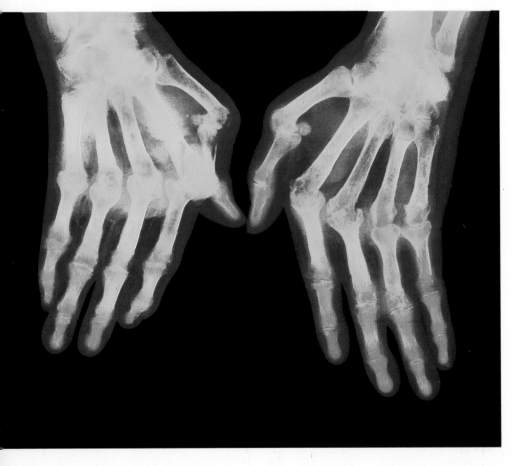

This X-ray image shows the hands of a person with rheumatoid arthritis. Some doctors and scientists think that allergy to some foods may be a factor in rheumatoid arthritis.

This man is making up a Chinese herbal treatment, which uses phytochemicals to prevent and treat disease.

These substances are called phytochemicals. They include allium compounds in onions, garlic, and chives; flavonoids in most fruits, vegetables, tea, and red wine; limonene found in oranges, lemons, and grapefruit; and diothiolthiones found in broccoli, Brussels sprouts, cabbage, and cauliflower.

DID YOU KNOW?

★ Levels of heart disease and cancer are very low in Italy, Spain, Greece, and other countries around the Mediterranean Sea. This is because the people there eat a very healthy diet containing lots of fruits and vegetables, a little fish, lean meat, olive oil, and a small amount of wine.

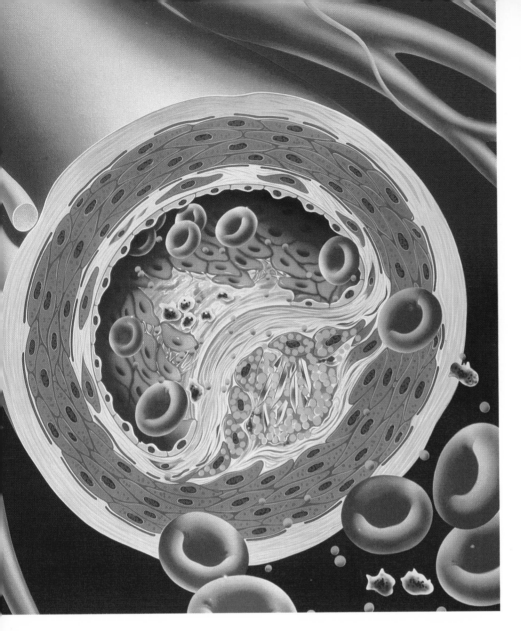

In heart disease, large blood vessels called arteries become clogged with a waxy, fatty substance called cholesterol (colored yellow in the picture). Consuming too many saturated and trans fats can raise cholesterol levels.

DIABETES

If you have diabetes, the pancreas gland in your body does not make enough insulin. Insulin is a substance that controls your body's blood sugar levels. Some people with diabetes have to inject themselves with insulin, but the food they eat is also very important in making sure that their blood sugar levels do not go too high or too low. People with diabetes need a diet that is high in complex carbohdyrates and fiber and low in sugar and fat.

HEART DISEASE

For a healthy heart you should eat plenty of fruits and vegetables. They are rich in vitamins that help keep blood vessels called arteries from clogging up with cholesterol, which is one of the causes of heart attacks. Butter, cream, fatty meats, and foods high in saturated and trans fats also raise cholesterol levels, so keep them to a minimum. Being overweight increases the risk of heart disease, so eat a healthy, low-fat diet and get enough exercise to maintain a healthy weight.

PROTECTION AGAINST CANCER

Cancer is a serious disease that occurs when some of the cells in your body divide and grow faster than they should. Experts think that eating properly can protect you against some kinds of cancer.

Make sure your diet gives you plenty of ACE vitamins and fiber. Avoid eating too many animal fats and go easy on foods like bacon, salami, and smoked meats. They are preserved with substances that have been linked to stomach cancer. Try not to eat barbecued food. Burning can produce harmful substances that could cause cancer.

THE ORGANIC OPTION

Many chemicals are sprayed on farm crops, including fertilizers to help them grow and pesticides to stop insects eating them. It is not known if these chemicals cause cancer, but many experts believe it is healthier to eat organic food, which is produced without the use of such chemicals.

Barbecued foods contain high levels of chemicals produced by burning that have been linked to bowel and other forms of cancer.

VEGETARIANISM

If you are vegetarian you do not eat meat, poultry, game, fish, or animal products such as gelatine and lard. Most vegetarians eat cheese, milk, yogurt, and eggs, which are produced by animals. Vegans are vegetarians who avoid all animal products.

WHY BE VEGETARIAN?

People are vegetarian for many different reasons, perhaps because they are worried about cruelty to animals, or because their religion forbids them to eat meat. Others are vegetarian simply because they do not like the taste of meat. Many people choose a vegetarian diet because they believe that avoiding meat and meat products is better for their health.

GOOD HEALTH WITHOUT MEAT

A well-balanced, low-saturated-fat, high-fiber vegetarian diet is extremely healthy. Vegetarians have a lower risk of certain cancers, heart disease, and conditions such as kidney- and gallstones than non-vegetarians.

They also have less chance of developing diabetes and high blood pressure and are less likely to be overweight. Provided you eat a variety of foods, including grains and cereals, fruits and vegetables, beans and peas, nuts, seeds, and a small amount of fat, you will get all the nutrients you need— whether or not you consume animal products.

MEETING SPECIAL NEEDS

Vitamin B 12, an essential nutrient, is found only in animal foods. If you are vegan you will not get any in your diet. You can meet your body's need for B12 by eating margarine and other foods fortified with B 12 (that is, with B 12 specially added). Alternatively, you can take a vitamin B 12 supplement. Calcium is important when you are growing, so if you are vegetarian you should make sure you eat at least three servings of dairy foods or foods fortified with vitamin D and calcium every day.

Left Lacto-vegetarians avoid meat and meat products, poultry and fish, but include dairy products such as cheese and yogurt in their diet. Vegans, by contrast, avoid all foods containing animal products.

Right An appealing vegetarian meal of pasta, vegetables, and herbs. A well-balanced vegetarian diet can provide you with all the nutrients you need for good health.

WHY AVOID TOO MUCH JUNK FOOD?

Snacking is not a bad way to eat, as long as you choose nutritious snacks. But snacks from vending machines and fast-food restaurants are often "junk foods"—high in fats and sugars and low in vitamins and minerals. They are also high in sodium, which is found in salt. Too much sodium can cause a rise in blood pressure, which in turn is linked to heart disease.

A LITTLE OF WHAT YOU LIKE

Junk and fast foods are fine from time to time, but try not to eat too many. A baked potato topped with sour cream with a salad and fruit juice is healthier than a cheeseburger, french fries, and a soda. Popcorn (with no butter or salt) is healthier than snacks such as potato chips. Look at the back of packages to see what they contain. Choose those with the least fat, sugar, and salt.

The occasional cheeseburger will not do you any harm, but avoid eating too many, as they are high in sugar and fat.

SNACKING AND GRAZING

When your parents were children, they probably sat down to three "proper" meals a day. Today, eating habits are much more casual. Instead of eating breakfast, lunch, and dinner you may eat on and off throughout the day, a style of eating often called grazing or snacking. When you feel hungry or thirsty, you grab a snack or help yourself to a drink. The availability of fast foods, ready meals, and packaged snacks makes it easier to graze.

CHOOSE THE HEALTHY OPTION

In a fast-food restaurant or school cafeteria think before you order. Choose a balanced meal containing carbohydrate, protein, and vegetables. Think about the way the food is cooked—broiled or baked foods are better for you than fried foods.

FOOD	CHOOSE	LIMIT
Fish	Broiled or baked	Battered and deep fried
Chicken	Skinless and broiled	Coated and deep fried
Pizza	Vegetable toppings such as mushrooms, pepper, spinach	Fatty toppings such as sausage, bacon, or extra cheese
Vegetables and salads	Fresh, eaten raw or steamed	Creamy, fatty dressings and sauces containing mayonnaise and blue cheese
Potatoes	Baked	Fried skins, french fries
Drinks	Juice, water, low-fat milk shakes (small sizes)	Full-fat milk shakes, squashes, carbonated drinks (large sizes)
Desserts	Fresh fruit, yogurt, fruit salad	Doughnuts, apple pie, chocolate fudge cake, cream pies

*When helping yourself to a snack, make sure
you choose something healthy.*

Left Everybody needs a certain amount of body fat, but being overweight is linked to several serious diseases in adult life. The amount of skin that can be "pinched" with these large calipers tells a doctor about how much body fat the patient has.

Below Lack of activity combined with too many unhealthy snacks can make you put on more weight than is healthy.

WEIGHT-WATCHING

Being overweight makes it harder for you to run around. It may also make you short of breath and can put a strain on your joints. Adults who are overweight, or obese, are more likely to develop diabetes, high blood pressure, and heart disease. Obese women are more likely to develop breast cancer.

ARE YOU OVERWEIGHT?

Doctors use what is called a body-mass index (BMI) chart to check if people are overweight. If you are concerned that you may be overweight, consult your doctor. You may have a high BMI if you are very muscular because you exercise a lot. In this case, you are not overweight.

WHY DO YOU GAIN WEIGHT?

You may inherit the tendency to gain weight from your parents through your genes. Your genes can affect when you feel full, where your body stores fat, and how fast you burn energy. Body weight is also linked to eating habits and exercise levels. People often overeat if they are sad, angry, or bored. You are more likely to put on weight if you sit around a lot watching television.

ACHIEVING A HEALTHY WEIGHT

If you are overweight, make sure you eat a well-balanced diet. If you currently do little or no exercise, initially aim for at least 30 minutes of exercise each day, such as walking. Gradually build up your activity level as you get more fit.

CONTROLLING YOUR WEIGHT

At least twice a week, try to do some more vigorous exercise such as running, dancing, tennis, or swimming. As you are growing, it is usually best to try to maintain the same weight rather than actually try to lose it.

DID YOU KNOW?

★ Some adults are "apple shaped," which means that they store fat around their middle.
★ Others are "pear shaped" and store fat around their hips and thighs.
★ Apple-shaped people are more likely to develop heart disease than pear-shaped people.

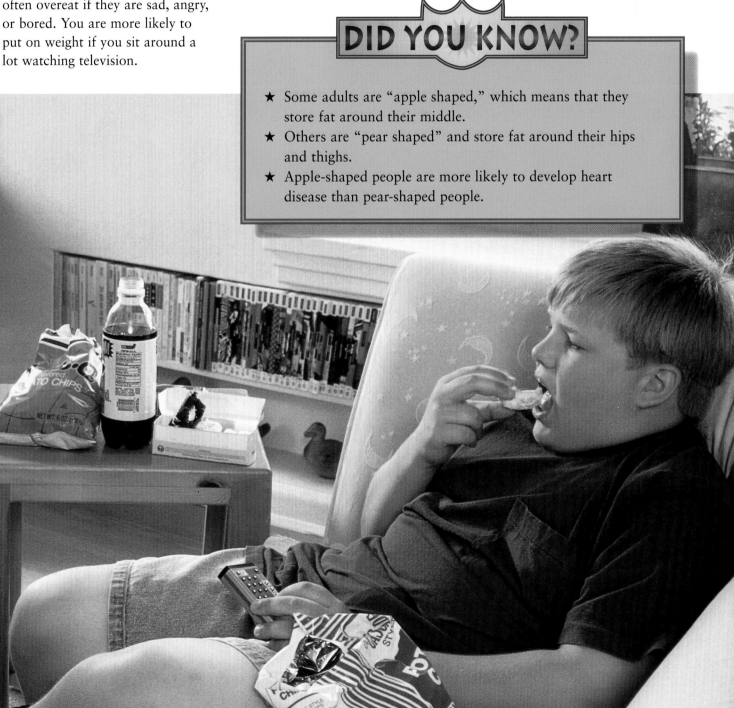

ARE YOU UNDERWEIGHT?

If you are naturally thin and wiry, you are probably perfectly healthy. However, if you do not weigh as much as you should because you have been severely cutting down on food, you could damage your health. Rapid, unexplained weight loss can be a sign of illness. Eating a balanced diet will ensure that you maintain a healthy weight.

If you eat well and exercise regularly, you will have plenty of energy and be the right weight for your age and height.

WHAT ARE EATING DISORDERS?

Eating disorders affect the way you think about food and what you eat. People with them are obsessed with what they look like, especially how much they weigh. People with anorexia nervosa deliberately do not eat enough and become severely underweight. Often they imagine they are fatter than they are. They feel so ashamed of the way they look they often avoid doing things like going to the gym or swimming, where they have to reveal their bodies.

Eating disorders may develop as a way of coping with problems. They can often be overcome with a counselor's help.

BINGE EATING

People with bulimia nervosa usually weigh the right amount but have no control over what they eat. They eat huge amounts in a short time. This is called a binge. It causes them to feel so bad that they make themselves sick. Sometimes they take laxatives (drugs that make you empty your bowels) or starve themselves to make up for bingeing.

COPING WITH EATING DISORDERS

If you have an eating disorder you need to find out what your correct weight should be and learn to eat healthily. You will also need the help and advice of an expert such as a doctor, dietitian, or counselor.

DIETARY TRAFFIC LIGHTS

STOP
Fatty and sugary foods to be limited
Fatty and fried foods: butter, margarine, lard, potato chips, french fries, fried vegetables, cream.
Sugary foods: jam, marmalade, honey, syrup, candy, chocolate, ice cream, cakes, cookies, puddings, pies and pastries, sweet drinks.

STEADY
Needed in moderate amounts for growth
Protein foods: lean meat, fish, eggs, cheese, baked beans, dried peas and beans, nuts.
Milk: skimmed or semi-skimmed.
Cereals: bread, cereal, pasta, rice.

Go
Nutritious foods to fill up on
Vegetables: raw, boiled, steamed, in salads.
Fruits: fresh, frozen, canned in juice.
Drinks: tea, coffee, water.
Seasonings: herbs, spices.

FOOD ALLERGIES

If eating a certain food frequently makes you have a rash, wheezing or sneezing, a headache, swelling or an upset stomach, you could have an allergy or a food intolerance. An allergy happens when your immune system, which protects you against disease, reacts to a substance that is normally harmless to your body. With a food intolerance, your body reacts to something you eat but the reaction does not involve your immune system.

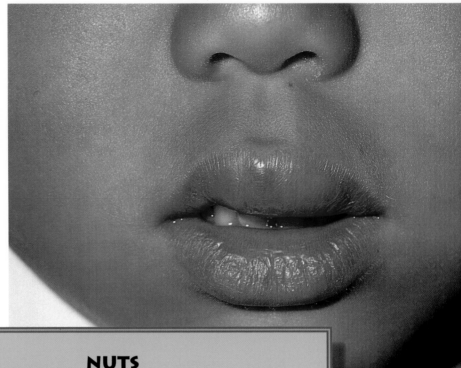

Below Peanuts are one of the most common causes of food allergy. Peanut oil is often used to make foods such as cookies and cakes.

NUTS

Some people are allergic to nuts, especially peanuts, walnuts, and cashew nuts. Eating even a small amount of nut, such as a cookie made with peanut oil, can cause their tongues, lips, and throats to swell up or bring on a severe asthma attack. Sometimes the reaction is so severe the person goes into a serious kind of shock, called anaphylactic shock, and may die. People who are at risk carry a vial containing a hormone called adrenaline, which can stop the reaction.

Above This boy's swollen upper lip is caused by an allergic reaction to eating peanuts.

ALLERGIES IN CHILDREN

People of all ages are affected by allergies, but they are particularly common in childhood. You may be among the one in three children who have an allergy such as asthma, eczema, hay fever or urticaria (a red, raised rash). Foods are one cause of allergies. The main culprits are milk and dairy products, wheat, eggs, shellfish, nuts, soy beans, and some additives and colorings found in processed foods.

AVOIDING ALLERGIES

If you think you are allergic to something you eat, the doctor can do a test to check which food may be causing the trouble. He or she may then advise you to stop eating that food altogether. After a time, you may be able to reintroduce small amounts of the food into your diet. You should only exclude a particular food or type of food from your diet if you are advised to do so by your doctor or a dietitian.

ALLERGY-CAUSING FOODS

Food	Possible symptoms
Milk and dairy products such as milk, butter, ice cream, cheese, yogurt	Diarrhea, constipation, migraine (a type of headache), pain in the abdomen, eczema
Gluten found in flour, and bread, cookies, canned and packaged soups, stock cubes, and processed foods	Migraine and coeliac disease, which causes diarrhea, weight loss, and anaemia
Eggs, usually the white part used in cakes, meringues, mayonnaise, and ice cream	Rashes, swelling, stomach upsets, asthma, eczema
Shellfish such as shrimp, crabs, and mussels	Stomachaches, migraine, nausea (feeling sick)
Nuts, especially peanuts, walnuts, cashews; also in nut bread, cookies and candy, ice cream and oils	Rashes, swelling, asthma, eczema. In severe cases, anaphylactic shock
Some additives, colorings and flavorings found in processed foods	Wheezing and other allergic reactions; some experts believe they may cause hyperactivity, behavior and learning difficulties

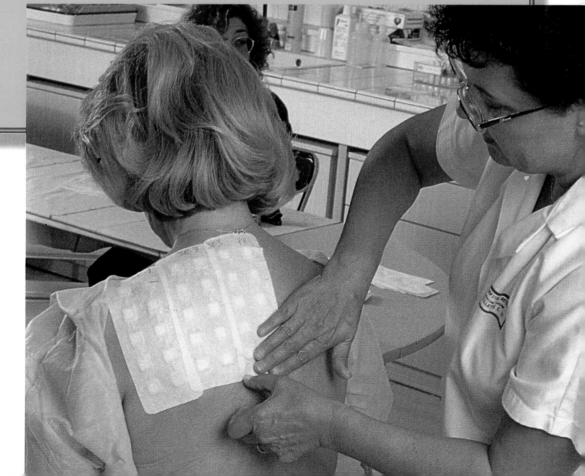

This woman is having a patch test to identify exactly what the cause of her allergy is. Small amounts of different substances are applied to her skin to see if they produce mildly allergic reactions. Food allergies are usually tested by omitting certain foods from a person's diet.

GLOSSARY

Allergy A reaction by your immune system to food or other usually harmless substances such as pollen, dust, feathers, or fur.

Amino acids The building blocks of proteins. There are about 20 amino acids, which join together to make many different proteins.

Anemia A condition in which the blood's level of hemoglobin—a type of protein that carries oxygen—is low. This reduces the supply of oxygen to the body's tissues.

Antioxidant A substance or nutrient that mops up free radicals, making them harmless. Vitamins A, C, E, and the minerals iron, zinc, copper, manganese, and selenium are antioxidants.

Carbohydrate A type of major nutrient needed by the body for energy. Simple carbohydrates have small molecules, while complex carbohydrates have large molecules.

Cartilage Flexible tissue, made of protein, that supports the skeleton.

Cells Tiny, living units that make up the human body. There are many different types of cells—such as nerve cells, blood cells, and muscle cells—each designed to carry out a specific task.

Cholesterol A waxy substance formed by the liver and present in foods such as egg yolks and animal fats. When cholesterol builds up in the arteries it can block them, leading to heart disease.

Fat A major type of nutrient that is stored in the body's tissues for use as energy. Fats contain more energy than carbohydrates but cannot be used as easily.

Fiber Parts of food, especially fruit and vegetables, that are difficult or impossible to digest but important for health. Insoluble fiber is found in cereal husks. Soluble fiber is found in the cell walls of plants.

Free radicals Molecules produced by the body's metabolism. Free radicals react with other molecules and can attack and damage cells. They have been linked to a number of diseases, including cancer and heart disease. Cigarette smoke, stress, illness, sunlight and other factors can cause overproduction of free radicals.

Genes Characteristics are passed on from parents to children by genes—chemical instructions carried inside the body's cells.

Growth spurt The increase in height and weight that comes before adolescence.

Immune system The cells and substances in the body that protect it against disease and bad health.

Metabolism The normal chemical processes that occur in the body.

Mineral A type of minor nutrient needed by the body for many vital processes. Iron and calcium are both important minerals.

Nutrients Substances found in food, which the body needs to stay healthy. The three main nutrients—fat, protein, and carbohydrate—are known as macronutrients. Vitamins, minerals, and other nutrients needed by the body in small quantities are known as micronutrients.

Oils Fats that are liquid at room temperature.

Phytochemicals Substances found in plants, vegetables, herbs, and fruits, which actively protect the body against disease.

Protein A type of major nutrient. Proteins consists of amino acids joined together. Their many jobs include growth and muscle formation and chemical reactions in the body's cells.

Starch A complex carbohydrate found in foods such as potatoes and cereals.

Sugar A simple carbohydrate found in fruit, candy, and other foods. The body can break down sugar more quickly than starch.

Tissue Cells of the same kind are grouped together to form material called tissue. Bones, cartilage, and muscles are all made of different types of tissue.

Vitamins Nutrients that the body needs in small quantities to control chemical reactions in cells. Vitamins also actively protect against certain diseases such as heart disease and cancer.

FURTHER INFORMATION

FURTHER READING

D'Amico, Joan. *The Healthy Body Cookbook: Over 50 Fun Activities and Delicious Recipes for Kids.* New York: John Wiley & Sons, 1999.

Buchanan, Peggy. *Movin' and Groovin': Fun Exercises to Do Any Time and Any Place.* Santa Barbara, CA: Learning Works, 1997.

Klaven, Ellen, ed. *The Vegetarian Fact Finder.* Little Bookroom, 1997.

Vancleave, Janice. *Janice Vancleave's Food and Nutrition for Every Kid: Easy Activities That Make Learning Science Fun.* New York: John Wiley & Sons, 1999.

USEFUL ADDRESSES

Kellogg Company
P.O. Box CAMB
Battle Creek, MI 49016-1986
Tel: (800) 962-1413
Web page:
www.kelloggs.com
Nutritional information.

United States Department of Agriculture
14th and Independence Ave. SW
Washington, D.C. 20250
Tel: (202) 720-2791
Web page: www.usda.gov
The USDA supports sustainable agriculture in order to enhance the quality of life for Americans. Among other things, the USDA advocates for farmers and sets standards for food growth and production. They publish a variety of newsletters and brochures, each focusing on a different topic, like nutrition and diet.

National Dairy Council
10255 West Higgins
Suite 900
Rosemont, IL 60018
Tel: (800) 426-8271
Web page:
www.nationaldairycouncil.org
The National Dairy Council's web page contains the latest news about health research, along with general information about nutrition. You can also get lots of recipes with milk and cheese, and take their Nutrition Quiz.

Family Food Zone
Web site:
www.familyfoodzone.com
This is an entertaining and informative web site for parents. There is a food guide, which includes an explanation of the food pyramid, shopping tips, and recipes that kids can make by themselves.

Food and Drug Administration
FDA (HFE-88)
5600 Fishers Lane
Rockville, MD 20857
Tel: (888) INFO-FDA
Web page: www.fda.gov
The Food and Drug Administration issues guidelines for the production of food and drugs in order to protect the health and rights of Americans. Their Web site contains information about food and drug regulations, consumer protection, and special information for women and children.

Vegetarian Resource Group
P.O. Box 1463
Baltimore, MD 21203
(410) 366-8343
www.vrg.org
This organization provides a wealth of information for vegetarians and vegans. They publish a newsletter, VRG News, and include vegetarian recipes, nutritional information, and travel guides on their Web site.

INDEX